CELEBRATING

DÍA DE LOS MUERTOS

BY ANN HEINRICHS · ILLUSTRATED BY MERNIE GALLAGHER-COLE

The Child's World®
childsworld.com

Published by The Child's World®
1980 Lookout Drive • Mankato, MN 56003-1705
800-599-READ • www.childsworld.com

ISBN 9781503853805 (Reinforced Library Binding)
ISBN 9781503854635 (Portable Document Format)
ISBN 9781503855014 (Online Multi-user eBook)
LCCN: 2021953064

Printed in the United States of America

ABOUT THE AUTHOR
Ann Heinrichs lives in Chicago, Illinois. She has written more than two hundred books for children. She loves traveling to faraway places.

ABOUT THE ILLUSTRATOR
Mernie Gallagher-Cole has illustrated many books for children. She lives in West Chester, Pennsylvania, with her husband Rick, daughter Glenna, and son Ian.

CONTENTS

CHAPTER 1

The Day of the Dead

Skeletons dance in the windows. Children eat candy shaped like skulls. Tables are heaped with flowers and food. It's Día de los Muertos (DEE-ah day lohs MWEHR-tohs)!

Día de los Muertos is Spanish for "day of the dead." But it's not a sad holiday. It's full of joy! It's a time to celebrate loved ones who have died.

People in Mexico celebrate Día de los Muertos. So do people in other parts of Central America and South America. Mexican Americans celebrate this holiday, too.

Día de los Muertos is a joyous festival!

CHAPTER 2

How It All Began

Aztec people once lived in Mexico. They held a festival to celebrate the dead. It lasted a whole month.

The Aztecs believed the spirits of the dead returned at this time. People rejoiced that their loved ones were visiting. They celebrated and danced. Skulls were part of the festival, too. They were **symbols** of death and rebirth.

Spanish people arrived in the 1500s. They were shocked at this festival. Spaniards saw death as the end of life. It was a time to be **grim**.

The Aztecs honored the goddess Mictecacihuatl (meek-tay-kah-SEE-hwahtl) at their festival of the dead. She was called the Lady of the Dead. The Aztecs believed she ruled the underworld.

The Aztecs' festival celebrated the cycle of life.

But the Aztecs had a different view. To them, death was part of the cycle of life. They watched this **cycle** every year. Their crops sprouted, grew, ripened, and died. Then the cycle began again.

CHAPTER 3

The Festival That Lived On

The Spaniards were Christians. They taught their religion to the Aztecs. But they could not change the Aztecs' celebration of the dead. Instead, they joined it with Christian beliefs.

November 2 is All Souls' Day. This Christian feast honors the dead. Among the people of Mexico, it became Día de los Muertos.

The Aztecs' old beliefs did not die. People still believed the spirits visited on Día de los Muertos. And the living still rejoiced!

Spaniards taught Christianity to the Aztecs, Mayans, and many other people from Mexico, Central America, and South America.

The Aztecs and Spaniards combined their beliefs to create Día de los Muertos.

Día de los Muertos is a three-day festival.

October 31st — Halloween

November 1st — All Saints' Day

November 2nd — All Souls' Day

CHAPTER 4

Three Days of Celebration

Día de los Muertos became a three-day festival. People begin celebrating on October 31, or Halloween. November 1 is the Christian feast of All Saints' Day. November 2 is All Souls' Day. These last two days are the main part of the Día de los Muertos celebration.

Día de los Muertos is very different from Halloween. Halloween treats death as scary. But Día de los Muertos is a happy time. It celebrates a loved one's life. And it laughs at death!

Children who have died are called *angelitos* (ahn-heh-LEE-tohs). That's Spanish for "little angels." Their spirits are believed to return on November 1.

CHAPTER 5

Visiting Graves

On Día de los Muertos, people believe that the spirits of the dead return. The spirits visit with family members and friends who are still alive.

People who have lost loved ones look forward to Día de los Muertos. They believe the spirits of their dead family and friends return to visit.

Yellow marigolds are known as the flowers of the dead. They have a strong, sweet smell. That helps the spirits find their way home.

This is a time to visit a loved one's grave. People clean and repaint the gravestone. They place marigolds and other flowers around it. Candles are lit around the grave, too.

People often visit a loved one's grave during *Día de los Muertos.*

People sometimes gather for a picnic during *Día de los Muertos. It is not unusual for this picnic to be at a loved one's grave.*

Friends and family members gather there. They tell stories about the person. They laugh and remember happy times. Often they have a picnic around the grave. They pray for their loved one, too. People may stay by the grave all through the night.

CHAPTER 6
Altars and Offerings

People prepare their homes for Día de los Muertos. They set up **altars** to the dead. The altar welcomes the loved one home.

Photos of the person are placed on the altar. The photos show the people as they were when they were young and happy. Candles and flowers adorn the altar. Incense is burned there, too.

Many *ofrendas* (oh-FREHN-dahs), or offerings, are placed on the altar. They help the spirit find its way home. Ofrendas might include the person's favorite objects. If the person was a child, there are toys. Favorite foods are set out. So are bread and skull-shaped candy.

The altar itself is sometimes called the ofrenda.

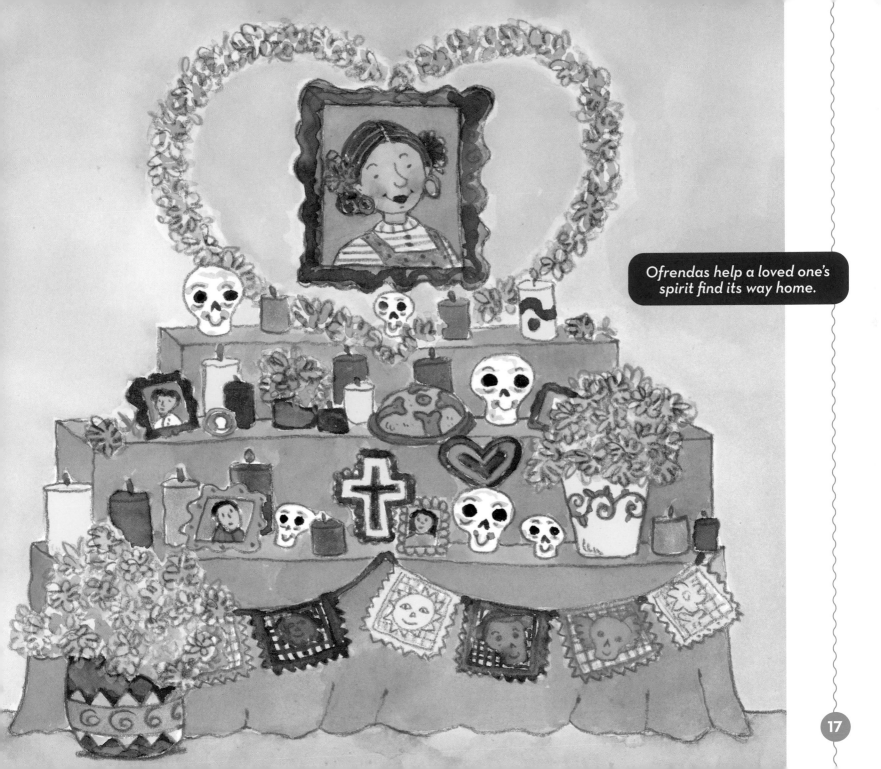

Ofrendas help a loved one's spirit find its way home.

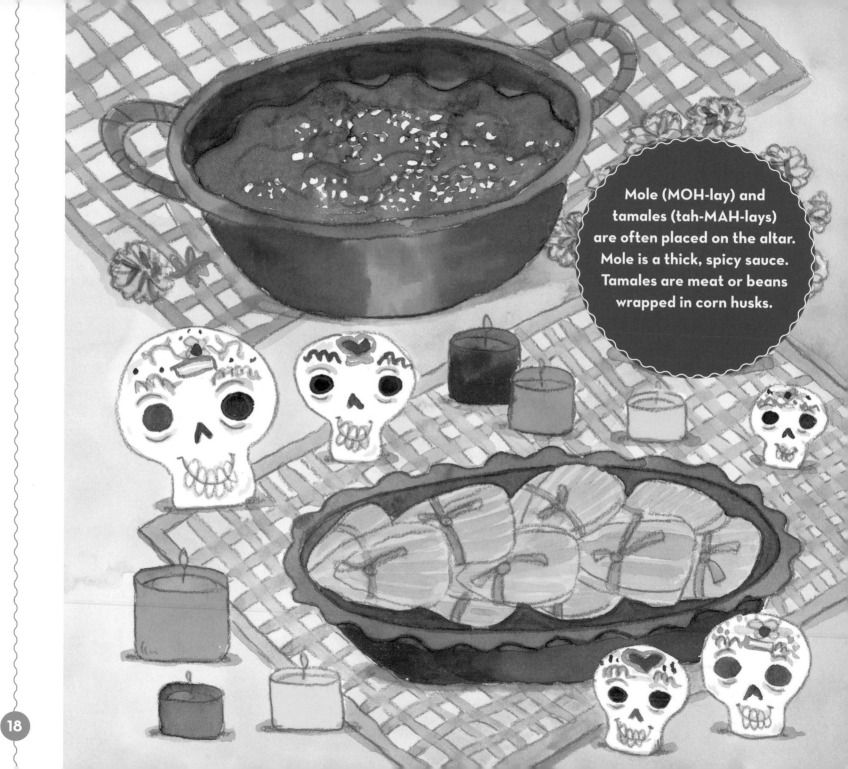

Mole (MOH-lay) and
tamales (tah-MAH-lays)
are often placed on the altar.
Mole is a thick, spicy sauce.
Tamales are meat or beans
wrapped in corn husks.

Colorful paper is hung above the altar. It's called *papel picado* (pah-PELL pee-KAH-doh). The paper is cut in pretty designs.

CHAPTER 7

Happy Skeletons

Skeletons are everywhere during Día de los Muertos. They are called *calacas* (kah-LAH-kahs). Skeleton pictures are favorite decorations.

What are the skeletons doing? Having fun! They are laughing or dancing. Some wear fancy clothes and jewelry. Huge, flowered hats sit atop their heads.

Skeleton figures are placed on altars. They're funny and playful. They may be relaxing in a chair or playing games. Or they might be working at what was once the dead person's job.

Calacas figures are sometimes called *calaveras* (kah-lah-VEH-rahs).

People often celebrate Día de los Muertos with a skeleton dance.

Día de los Muertos often includes a skeleton dance. People put on skull masks. Then they dance around gaily. It's a way of laughing at death!

CALAVERAS POEM

Spanish:

Ahí viene el agua
Por la ladera,
Y se me moja
Mi calavera.

La muerte calaca,
Ni gorda ni flaca.
La muerte casera,
Pegada con cera.

English:

Here comes the water
Down the slope
And my skull
Is getting wet.

Death, a skeleton
Neither fat nor skinny.
A homemade skeleton
Stuck together with wax.

—Traditional

CHAPTER 8

Food for the Dead

There are special foods for Día de los Muertos. One is *pan de muerto* (PAHN day MWER-toh). That means "bread of the dead." It's usually a round loaf. The icing on top looks like bones and skulls. A tiny, fake skeleton may be inside.

Another food is *calaveritas* (kah-lah-veh-REE-tahs). Those are skull-shaped candies. They're mostly made of sugar. A dead person's name is on each piece. Both pan de muerto and calaveritas are placed on the altars. They are sweet treats for the dead!

Mexicans have many sayings about death. One is: *La muerte es flaca y no ha de poder conmigo.* That's Spanish for "Death is skinny (or weak) and has no power over me."

Calaveritas is Spanish for "little skulls."

JOINING IN THE SPIRIT OF DÍA DE LOS MUERTOS

* Do you know a Mexican American? Ask him or her about family celebrations for Día de los Muertos.

* Is there a Mexican neighborhood in your community? Find out if it holds a Día de los Muertos festival. If so, go and enjoy the colorful sights!

* Write a poem about funny skeletons. Can you see how skeletons don't have to be scary?

* Find an easy recipe for sugar candy. Have a grown-up help you make it. Shape the candy into little skulls.

MAKING A DÍA DE LOS MUERTOS VEGETABLE SKELETON

What you need:

1 cucumber
1 tomato
1 black olive
1 green pepper or red pepper
2 cups carrot sticks
1/2 cup low-fat dip or salad dressing

Directions

1. Dice the cucumber and tomato into wedges, and slice the olive into smaller rings.*

2. Cutting from the top downward, divide the pepper in half. Place the pepper on a serving platter so that the inside is face down.

3. Arrange the carrot sticks, cucumber, and tomato to create arms, legs, ribs, and other bones.

4. Use a little of the low-fat dip or salad dressing to stick the olive rings to the pepper for eyes, a mouth hole, and a nose hole.

5. Your creation is sure to be a colorful Día de los Muertos offering! Don't forget to celebrate this joyful festival by sampling the various parts of your skeleton with the leftover dip or dressing.

*Have an adult help you with the cutting.

MAKING A PASTA SKELETON

What you need:
Uncooked dry pasta in different shapes
    (wagon wheels, macaroni, spirals,
    spaghetti, etc.)
1 piece of black construction paper
Glue
1 white crayon

Directions

1. Place pasta shapes on the black construction paper to form a skeleton. Don't glue them down until you have the skeleton laid out. Be sure it looks like you want it to. Also be sure it fits on the paper!

2. Glue the pasta on the paper one piece at a time.

3. Let the glue dry completely.

4. Use the white crayon to write your name or to give your skeleton a name.

Place the skeleton on your ofrenda and enjoy the holiday!

GLOSSARY

altars (ALL-turz)—tables set up for religious devotion

cycle (SY-kull)— set of events that keeps repeating

grim (GRIM)—gloomy

symbols (SIM-bullz)—objects, images, or words that stand for an idea

LEARN MORE

BOOKS

Barner, Bob. *The Day of the Dead: A Bilingual Celebration.* New York : Holiday House, 2011.

De Llano, Berta. *Citlali and the Day of the Dead | Citlali y el Dia de Muertos.* Greensboro, NC: Brighter Child, 2020.

Eliot, Hannah. *Día de Los Muertos.* New York, NY: Little Simon, 2018.

Thong, Roseanne Greenfield. *Día de Los Muertos.* Chicago, IL: Albert Whitman & Company, 2020.

Tonatiuh, Duncan. *Funny Bones: Posada and His Day of the Dead Calaveras.* New York, NY : Abrams, 2015.

WEBSITES

Visit our website for links about Día de los Muertos:
childsworld.com/links

Note to Parents, Teachers, and Librarians: We routinely verify our Web links to make sure they are safe and active sites. So encourage your readers to check them out!

INDEX